# REAL MONSTERS

# TASMANIAN DEVIL

## SAVAGE ISLAND SCAVENGER

**MARCIA AMIDON LUSTED**

Checkerboard Library

An Imprint of Abdo Publishing
abdopublishing.com

**ABDOPUBLISHING.COM**

Published by Abdo Publishing, a division of ABDO, PO Box 398166, Minneapolis, Minnesota 55439. Copyright © 2017 by Abdo Consulting Group, Inc. International copyrights reserved in all countries. No part of this book may be reproduced in any form without written permission from the publisher. Checkerboard Library™ is a trademark and logo of Abdo Publishing.

Printed in the United States of America, North Mankato, Minnesota
092016
012017

Design: Christa Schneider, Mighty Media, Inc.
Production: Mighty Media, Inc.
Editor: Liz Salzmann
Cover Photo: Shutterstock Images
Interior Photos: Alamy, pp. 12, 13, 21, 24; Getty Images, p. 27; iStockphoto, pp. 9, 10, 11, 15, 16, 19; Mighty Media, Inc., pp. 7, 17; Shutterstock Images, pp. 4, 6, 7, 20, 23, 25, 29; Torsten Blackwood/AFP/Getty Images, p. 28

**Publisher's Cataloging-in-Publication Data**
Names: Lusted, Marcia Amidon, author.
Title: Tasmanian devil : savage island scavenger / by Marcia Amidon Lusted.
Other titles: Savage island scavenger
Description: Minneapolis, MN : Abdo Publishing, 2017. | Series: Real monsters |
    Includes bibliographical references and index.
Identifiers: LCCN 2016944857 | ISBN 9781680784237 (lib. bdg.) |
    ISBN 9781680797763 (ebook)
Subjects:  LCSH: Tasmanian devils--Juvenile literature.
Classification: DDC 599.2/7--dc23
LC record available at http://lccn.loc.gov/2016944857

# CONTENTS

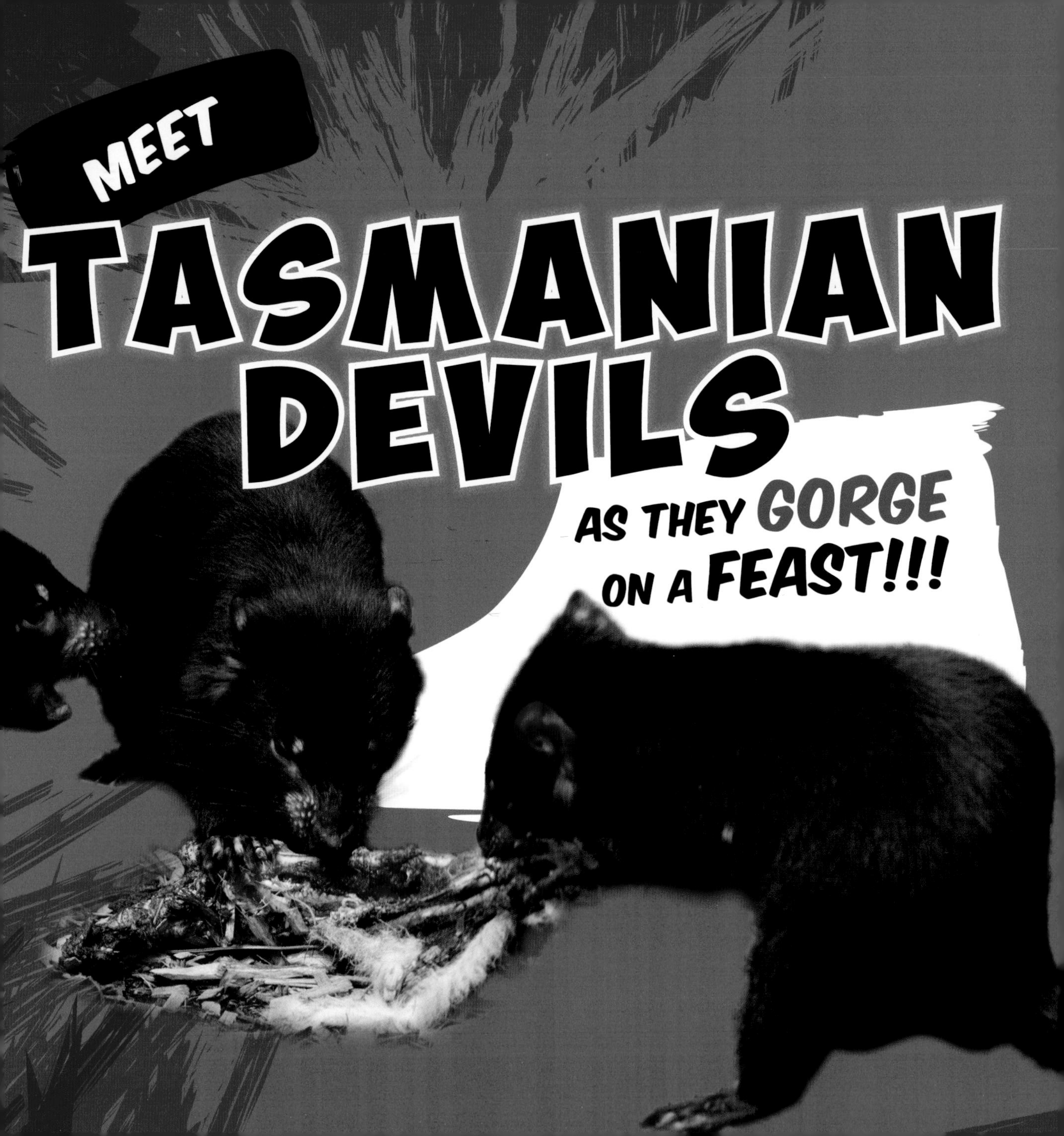
MEET
TASMANIAN DEVILS
AS THEY GORGE ON A FEAST!!!

A dead wallaby lies in a clearing. A Tasmanian devil picks up its scent and seeks out the meal. But it is not the only one.

Several other Tasmanian devils have also reached the carcass. The clearing echoes with their screeches and growls. This is how the devils show dominance as they dine.

With a high-pitched scream, the newcomer pushes in to share the feast. The commotion continues as the devils tear at the wallaby. Soon there is nothing left, not even fur or bones.

# CREATURE FEATURE

**NAME:** Tasmanian devil

**NICKNAMES:** The devil, Beelzebub's pup

**CLASS:** Mammalia

**SIZE:** 20 to 31 inches (51 to 79 cm) long

**WEIGHT:** 9 to 26 pounds (4 to 12 kg)

**COLORATION:** black or dark brown with white patches on chest and rear

**LIFE SPAN:** 7 to 8 years

## MONSTROUS CHARACTERISTICS

> Sharp teeth and claws

> Powerful jaws

> Loud screams, screeches, and growls

> Foul odor

> Bright red ears when angry or afraid

INDIAN OCEAN

N
W · E
S

AUSTRALIA

 Tasmanian Devil Range

TASMANIA

SOUTHERN OCEAN

> Range: Tasmania
> Diet: Birds, lizards, amphibians, insects, fish, **carrion**

**FUN FACT**
The Tasmanian devil is the world's largest carnivorous marsupial.

# FROM ANIMAL TO DEVIL

**H**ow does an animal the size of a small dog get such a fierce name? Tasmania is an island off the Australian coast. A story told by the island's **aborigines** explains why. In the story, the animal was called Taraba and was handsome. It had large eyes and soft, curling hair on its tail. But it was a nasty creature that ate baby animals.

There were powerful Spirit Helpers who lived in the **bush**. They helped look after the creatures in the wild. One day, Taraba accidentally reached into the Spirit Helpers' home looking for baby animals. The Spirit Helpers were angry. They changed the animal so it was no longer handsome. It grew long claws and an ugly snout. It lost its curly fur. From then on, it was named "devil."

In the early 1800s, Europeans traveled to the island of Tasmania. There, they ran into these fierce creatures. The Europeans didn't know what the locals called the animal. So, they came up with their own name

A Tasmanian devil's teeth continue to grow slowly throughout its life.

for it.  They noted its menacing display of sharp teeth and heard its chilling growl and screams.  Then they too decided to call the animal "devil."

## THE FAMOUS TAZ

Many people know about Tasmanian devils because of a cartoon character.  Taz appeared in "Looney Tunes" cartoons that were popular in the 1990s.  However, Taz and real Tasmanian devils do not have much in common.

Taz is tan and brown.  He is seen during the day and travels around the world.  A real Tasmanian devil is black or dark brown.  It only comes out to hunt at night.  And it is only found in Tasmania.

The Tasmanian devil's fierce behaviors are most often just for show.  They are a way for it to defend its food and warn off other Tasmanian devils.  Its wide-open mouth actually expresses fear or uncertainty.  Its screams and growls tell other devils that it is the leader.

The Tasmanian devil also produces a bad-smelling scent.  It releases this foul scent when it is **stressed**.  The scent's purpose is also to **deter** animals from getting close.

These **repellent** behaviors usually work to scare rivals away.  Tasmanian devils avoid fights that might cause serious injuries to each other.  However, male Tasmanian devils do fight one another during mating season to gain attention from females.

When two devils meet nose-to-nose, one usually backs down.

# A ROUGH START

Tasmanian devils mate between February and April each year. Baby devils are called imps or joeys. At first, each imp is the size of a grain of rice! Tasmanian devils are marsupials. The imps live in their mother's pouch after birth.

As many as 30 imps can be born in a litter. But the mother only has four **nipples**. So, only up to four imps survive. They each latch onto a nipple in her pouch with their claws and teeth.

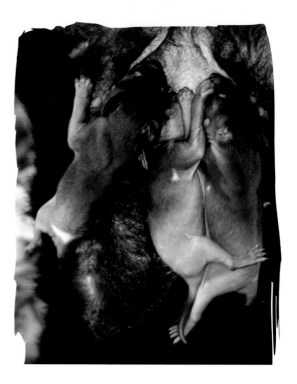

The imps may outgrow the mother's pouch. But they still latch onto her nipples.

**Young Tasmanian devils climb trees after leaving the den. This provides protection from predators.**

After four months, the imps leave the pouch. They either ride on their mother's back or stay in the den while she hunts. Devils are **weaned** at six months and become independent at nine months. They breed by the end of their second year and mate annually after that.

# COMMUNAL EATING

As they grow, young Tasmanian devils often play together. And adult devils often feed **communally**. However, these animals are **typically** solitary. They are also nocturnal. This means devils sleep during the day. They come out of their dens at night to hunt.

When hunting, Tasmanian devils use their powerful sense of smell to find food. They are mainly **scavengers**, eating what they find. This is usually wallaby, kangaroo, or wombat **carrion**. Or it might be a dead sheep or cow on a farm. Tasmanian devils also sometimes hunt live prey. They catch small mammals, birds, lizards, insects, and fish.

Often more than one Tasmanian devil will find the same carrion. That's when the

## ON THE RUN

A Tasmanian devil may travel up to ten miles (16 km) looking for food. The devil typically travels slowly. But when needed, it can pick up speed! Devils gallop with both hind feet together, reaching up to 15 miles per hour (24 kmh).

The devil is one of the only carnivores that lives alone but eats with others.

devilish displays of teeth, screaming, and growling begin. Usually two to five devils will share a meal. But large **carrion** can attract up to 12 of them.

They use their powerful teeth and jaws to eat every part of their meal, including bones. Tasmanian devils' consumption of carrion is helpful to the **environment**. The devils remove rotting carcasses and the flies that come with them.

Tasmanian devils are gorge feeders. This means that they eat a lot of food at a time. They can eat 40 percent of their body weight in a single day! And like other marsupials, the Tasmanian devil stores extra fat in its tail. A fat, fleshy tail means that a devil has plenty of food.

**A devil typically passes food through its system within five to seven hours.**

# TASMANIAN DEVIL: PREDATOR, PREY, AND CLEAN-UP CREW

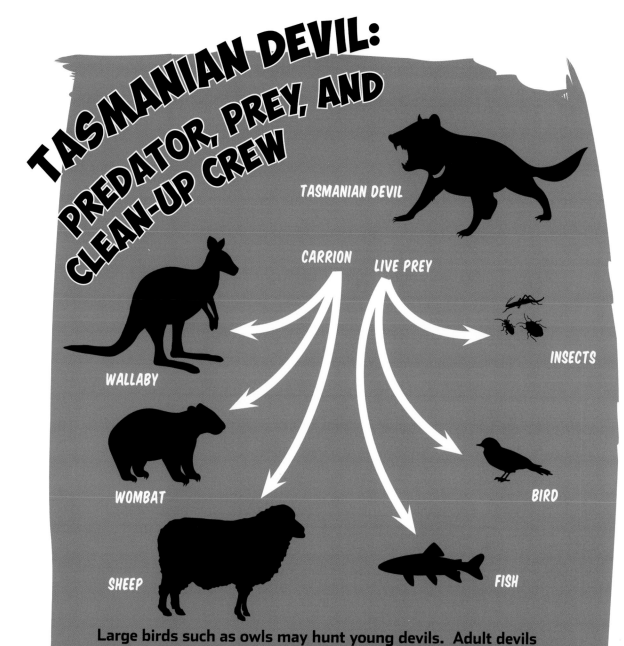

TASMANIAN DEVIL

CARRION    LIVE PREY

WALLABY

INSECTS

WOMBAT

BIRD

SHEEP

FISH

Large birds such as owls may hunt young devils. Adult devils have no natural predators. But they sometimes fight and kill one another. **Carrion** and smaller live prey are the devils' main diet. They also hunt wallabies and wombats that are sick and slow.

17

# HOME SWEET HOME

Long ago, Tasmanian devils lived throughout Australia. Between 3,500 and 5,000 years ago, dogs called dingoes were imported from Asia. Scientists believe dingoes and devils competed for food. This led to Tasmanian devils becoming extinct on the mainland. However, dingoes don't live on Tasmania. So today, devils are only found on this island.

Tasmanian devils live all over Tasmania. They will live anywhere that provides them shelter during the day and food at night. This includes **eucalyptus** forests, rain forests, and the **bush**. Devils can also be found near farms, where there might be farm animal carcasses to eat.

The devils make dens in burrows, bushes, thick clumps of grass, hollow logs, or caves. They will also dig their own dens. Each animal **typically** uses several dens. Some of their dens may have been used for hundreds of years.

Wild dingoes often mate with other types of dogs. Today, pure dingoes are rare.

Each Tasmanian devil establishes a home range. This is the area that it usually travels in. A devil's home range is about three to eight square miles (8 to 20 sq km). However, several devils may have **overlapping** ranges. When they do, they often have a shared bathroom area. This could be near a water hole or where well-used paths meet.

Tasmanian devils leave their dens just after dark. They follow specific routes, looking for food. Sometimes they lie in wait to catch live prey as it passes. Devils may roam and hunt all night. Then, they head back to their dens just before sunrise.

A Tasmanian devil doesn't always spend the entire day in its den. Sometimes it sleeps in the sun.

The only Tasmanian devils that share a den are a mother and her babies.

# DEVIL DANGER

**A**lthough adult Tasmanian devils have no natural predators, they have been hunted. In the 1800s, farmers killed many of these misunderstood creatures. The farmers thought the animals were killing their livestock.

Tasmanian devils did sometimes take **poultry** from farms, but never larger animals. And, the devils were actually helping the farmers. They ate the carcasses of dead sheep and cattle. This kept **maggots** from growing on the carcasses and hatching into blowflies. Blowflies can **infect** living animals. Today, most farmers are aware of this benefit. But in the past, hundreds of Tasmanian devils were trapped, poisoned, and shot by farmers.

**FUN FACT**
Because they eat almost anything, devils have been called "four-legged vacuum cleaners."

Today, infection from blowflies costs the Australian sheep industry more than $200 million a year.

In addition, the government of Tasmania began offering **bounties** for dead Tasmanian devils in 1830. It paid 25 cents for each male and 35 cents for each female. Over the next century, more and more of the animals were hunted and killed.

The Tasmanian devil almost became extinct. Then, in 1941, the government made the devil a protected species. This made killing them illegal. After that, their numbers began to increase.

Unfortunately, another threat developed for the Tasmanian devil. In the mid-1990s, scientists identified an illness called devil facial **tumor** disease (DFTD). It is a kind of rare **cancer** that is very **contagious**.

The cancer spreads quickly, forming lumps around the

**DFTD tumors make it hard for the devil to eat. Eventually the animal starves to death.**

**DFTD can be transmitted when a sick devil bites a healthy one.**

animal's face and mouth.  The **cancer** also spreads easily from animal to animal.  Tens of thousands of Tasmanian devils have been killed by DFTD since its discovery.  Scientists are worried about the effect this disease will have on the Tasmanian devil population.

# THE DEVIL'S FUTURE

The Tasmanian devil is an important part of the ecosystem in Tasmania. Removing **carrion** is just one of the things this animal does to benefit the **environment**. Tasmanian devils are also important for keeping the population of red foxes in control.

The red fox is responsible for the extinction of many native animals in Australia. But foxes aren't as big a problem in Tasmania. This is partly because they have to compete with Tasmanian devils for food and shelter. However, DFTD has reduced the number of Tasmanian devils in some areas. In those areas, the fox population is growing too quickly.

Because the Tasmanian devil is so important to Tasmania's ecosystem, humans are trying to help them. Scientists are working to find a way to fight DFTD. They are relocating some healthy Tasmanian devils to islands off the shores of Tasmania. They hope to create new healthy colonies of these animals.

Researchers capture and study devils to learn more about DFTD. Many devils are released back into the wild.

The Save the Tasmanian Devil Program is **sponsored** by the Australian government.  Its mission is to combat DFTD and keep Tasmanian devils from becoming extinct.  The Devil Island Project is another program working to protect these animals.  It is creating large fenced **sanctuaries**.  There, healthy Tasmanian devils can live in the wild, separated from devils with DFTD.

The Tasmanian devil doesn't deserve its reputation as a fierce monster.  This fascinating animal is vital to its **habitat**.  It is important to make sure that this misunderstood creature doesn't become one more extinct species.

**The Taronga Zoo in Australia works to breed Tasmanian devils that are resistant to DFTD.**

Biologists hope to start a population of devils free from DFTD on Maria Island, Australia, in the future.

# GLOSSARY

**aborigines** — the first or earliest-known people living in a certain area.

**bounty** — a reward offered for the capture of an animal.

**bush** — a large stretch of uncleared or mostly unsettled land covered with shrubby growth, especially in Australia.

**cancer** — any of a group of often deadly diseases marked by harmful changes in the normal growth of cells. Cancer can spread and destroy healthy tissues and organs.

**carrion** — dead, rotting animal flesh.

**communal** — shared by many.

**contagious** — spread by direct or indirect contact with an infected person or animal.

**deter** — to prevent or discourage.

**environment** — all the surroundings that affect the growth and well-being of a living thing.

**eucalyptus** — an evergreen tree originally from Australia that is now grown in many places.

**habitat** — a place where a living thing is naturally found.

**infect** — to enter and cause disease.

# WEBSITES

To learn more about Real Monsters,
visit **booklinks.abdopublishing.com**.
These links are routinely monitored and
updated to provide the most current
information available.

**maggot** — the larva of certain flies.

**nipple** — the raised part of a mammal's breast that provides milk to its young.

**overlap** — to occupy the same area in part.

**poultry** — birds raised on a farm for their meat and eggs.

**repellent** — causing disgust, or keeping or driving something away.

**sanctuary** — a refuge for wildlife where predators are controlled and hunting is illegal.

**scavenger** — a person or animal who searches through waste for something that can be used.

**sponsor** — to pay for a program or an activity.

**stress** — to feel physical, emotional, or mental strain.

**tumor** — an abnormal mass of cells in the body.

**typically** — generally or normally.

**wean** — to accustom an animal to eating food other than its mother's milk.

# INDEX